Old CARDONALD

by
Bill Spalding

Glasgow Corporation tramcar No.57 (service 32) in Paisley Road West at Halfway, September 1958. Behind the tram, the tenement at the far corner of Mosspark Boulevard has now vanished.

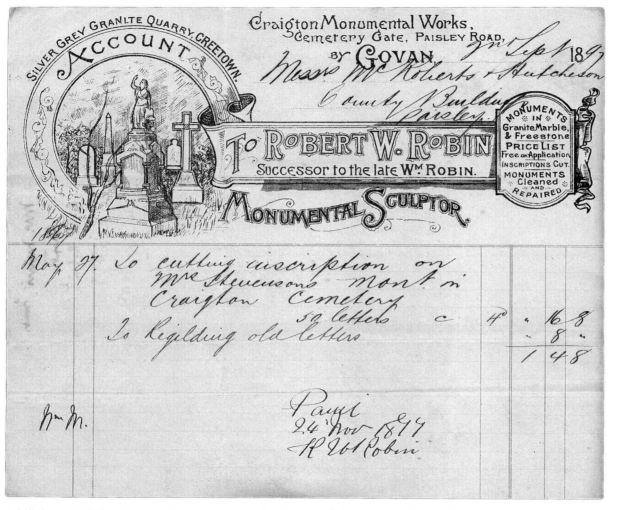

© Bill Spalding 1999
First published
in the United Kingdom, 1999,
by Stenlake Publishing,
Ochiltree Sawmill, The Lade,
Ochiltree, Ayrshire, KA18 2NX
Telephone / Fax: 01290 423114

ISBN 1 84033 082 1

THE PUBLISHERS REGRET
THAT THEY CANNOT SUPPLY
COPIES OF ANY PICTURES
FEATURED IN THIS BOOK.

ACKNOWLEDGEMENTS
The publishers wish to thank Robert Grieves for supplying the pictures on pages 28 and 29; Kenneth Binns and the management of Leverndale Hospital for permission to reproduce the picture on page 39; and Ian M. Symon for permission to reproduce the picture on page 40.

A bill from 1897 detailing work carried out by the Craigton Monumental Works. Over two hundred years old, Craigton Cemetery lies behind Halfway. When the old College Churchyard in High Street was removed, some of the remains from it were reinterred here.

Paisley Road Toll, Glasgow, looking West.

For centuries, traffic leaving Glasgow for Paisley and Renfrew went through the toll at Bridge Street and travelled along the road west before reaching the next toll which was at the present Paisley Road Toll. Here the road divided, with the fork on the right leading to Renfrew and the fork on the left leading to Paisley. There were stages for coaches on this stretch of road and the first was situated around the top of the present Broomloan Road. As it was roughly two miles from Glasgow it was called 'Two Mile House'. The next toll, 'Three Mile House', was known as 'Halfway' as it stood halfway between Glasgow and Paisley. It was also on the boundary between Govan Parish in Lanarkshire and Paisley Abbey Parish in Renfrewshire.

Before Paisley Road West was constructed in 1753, the route from Halfway continued up over the hills and along the line of the present Moss Heights, Wedderlea Drive, South Hillington Farm, Oldhall Farm and Arkleston Road, before reaching Paisley. For many years the route ran through open countryside containing a few large farms and the country residences of Glasgow businessmen, but by around 1905 when this photograph was taken, the area was becoming built-up.

In the early nineteenth century Halfway had cottages, an inn, a smithy and a school. Smithy records of 1839 to 1860 list customers such as Cardonald Mill, the Glasgow & Paisley Canal Company and the Hurlet Road Trustees. The school was the Three-Mile Subscription School which had been established on the death of one Richardson of Ralston in 1840. He left nearly £1,000 'to assist in erecting and maintaining in all time coming a school in the neighbourhood of the Three-Mile House'. There was no other school for two miles and due to lack of funds it was sometimes impossible to get a teacher to accept the position of schoolmaster. The pupils mostly came from Three-Mile House but some came from areas further afield including Ibrox, Hillington Toll and Crookston.

The post office has long since moved across the main road and most of the buildings on the left have been demolished. A supermarket stands on their site now.

Maryland Drive, *c.* 1903. The area just behind Halfway used to be called Marylands and Merrylands House stood close by on the main road to the east of Halfway. Further south at the Southern General Hospital was the area known as Merryflats which derived from Mireyflats, a reference to the marshy nature of the ground there. A mansion, Craigton House, was built close to Maryland Drive around 1746 and later the Dog and Cat Home was located in some of its buildings before it was transferred to Kinnell Avenue.

Cardonald School.

This view of Cardonald School was taken from the vacant site where the Post Office sorting office was later built. When the school was built in 1860, Cardonald was still in Renfrewshire and its full name was Paisley (Landward) Cardonald Public School (Renfrew). For a time children were also accepted from Corkerhill and from Crookston Home and this, plus the continued growth of Cardonald's population, resulted in the original building being extended in the 1890s.

For a time the Catholic population around Halfway was ministered by St Anthony's Parish at Govan Cross. Then they attended services in the convent at Maryland House. When Nazareth House was opened in 1906, Cardonald Catholic Mission was established and worship took place in the convent chapel. In 1922 the Mission's first church, Our Lady of Lourdes, was opened. With the development of Cardonald, Mosspark, Craigton, Bellahouston and Berryknowes from 1925, the church, seen here on the left, soon became too small and a new, larger building was opened in 1940, just off the picture to the right.

NAZARETH HOUSE, CARDONALD, GLASGOW.

In 1906 Nazareth House was opened as a 'Home for Destitute Orphans and Incurable Children and for Aged Men and Women'. It was a branch of Nazareth House, Hammersmith, and the aged poor were received without distinction as to creed or nationality.

NAZARETH HOUSE, CARDONALD, GLASGOW.

The building could accommodate 210 children and 37 old people and was run by the Sisters of Nazareth who had arrived in Cardonald in 1902 and who were initially based at Maryland House which still stands behind the Social Security offices at the corner of Paisley Road West and Corkerhill Road.

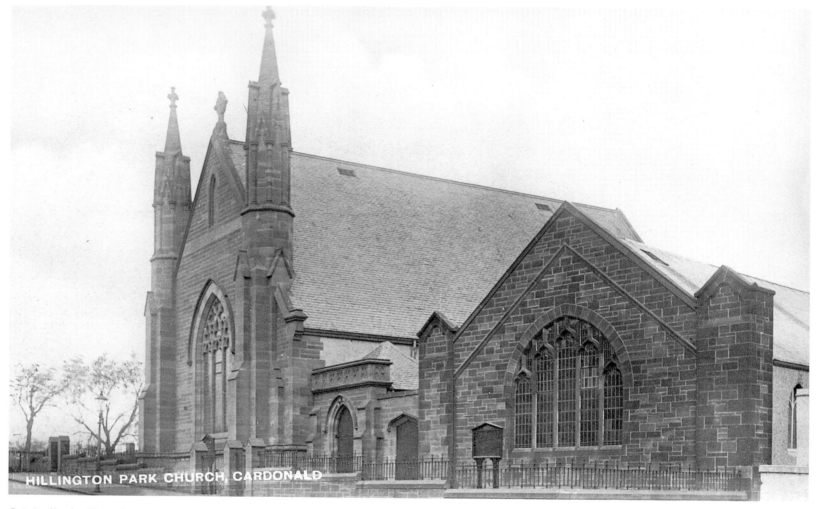

HILLINGTON PARK CHURCH, CARDONALD

Originally the United Free Church, this building was erected on Berryknowes Road in 1907. The site had previously been turned down for the Parish Church which was later built opposite Tweedsmuir Road.

The curved terrace of Hillington Park Circus contains some of the earliest houses built in Cardonald, with the site probably chosen because it is near Cardonald Railway Station. The street in the foreground, Wedderlea Drive, is now a dead end for vehicles, with concrete bollards at this point. The area between this terrace and Paisley Road West was at one time called Hillington Park.

These attractive houses in Hillington Gardens are little changed today. This postcard carried the caption 'City Gardens' but this may just have been a general description and not meant as the name of the street.

Midlothian & Lothian Gardens, Cardonald.

These two terraces were built on the south side of the main road. The area behind them was once known as Thistle Park. The tower of Hawkhead (Leverndale) Hospital can be seen rising in the middle distance.

A view of the bowling and tennis clubs taken when the Crookston & Cardonald main drainage tunnel was being constructed in 1928-29. On the far left is the railway line while in the foreground are the tracks for the bogies and the steam travelling crane used during construction of Shaft No. 10, as the tunnel was officially known.

Cardonald Bowling Green.

This postcard of the bowling green was posted in 1924 with the message 'They are very busy with the building of the Church. We will soon not know the place about here for new buildings.' The sender would have been referring to the east aisle extension to Cardonald Parish Church which opened in 1925. The bowling club still exists although the clubhouse has since been replaced by a new building.

A game in progress at the tennis courts with the ladies somewhat encumbered by the length of their skirts. After about fifty years the club closed down and the site is now occupied by a nursing home.

Traquair Road, Cardonald.

Initially called Carlyle Drive, the houses on Traquair Drive were built some time between 1898 and 1911. The vacant space halfway up on the right was taken by a telephone exchange in 1935, while the other one at the top on the left had houses built on it in the 1930s.

In this view a pithead frame stands on the corner of Hillhead (now Tweedsmuir) Road and Paisley Road West, where Safeway supermarket now stands. This was erected during the construction of the Crookston & Cardonald main drainage sewer tunnel. The white building in the background is Hillhead Farm.

Taken north of Cardonald at Shieldhall, this view of the sewage tunnel construction shows a steam travelling crane which handled excavated materials, trench timbers, bricks, concrete and other heavy loads.

Paisley Road, Cardonald.

Paisley Road West, *c.* 1934. The row of shops on the right are still there and were later joined by another row where the advertising hoardings stood. The hoardings on the opposite side of the road were removed to make way for the Aldwych Cinema in 1939. The Safeway supermarket currently stands on the site.

A 1930s view looking westwards. There is still a Shell garage tucked in between the Parish Church and the newsagents

Glasgow corporation tramcar No.191 (service 32) on Paisley Road West approaching the junction at Berryknowes Road in September 1958. Going from Crookston to Bishopbriggs, this is an example of the great length of some of the tramcar routes at that time.

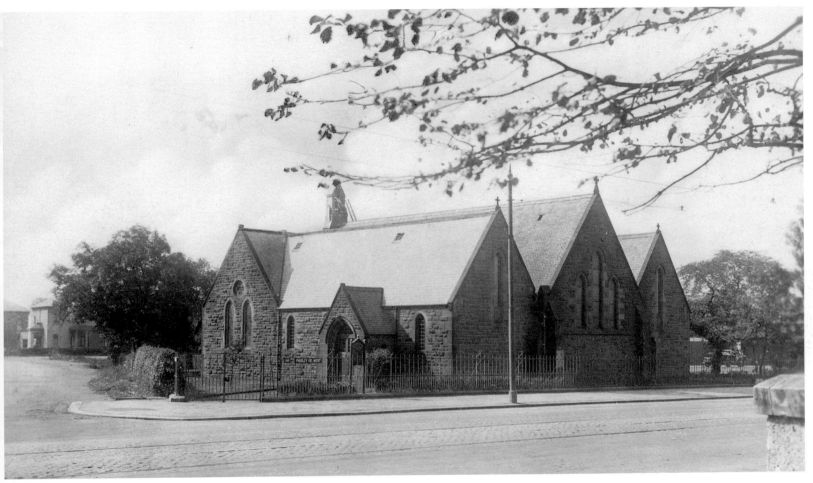

Prior to 1887 most residents of Cardonald were in the care of Paisley Abbey, while a smaller number belonged to Govan Parish. There was, however, a strong local desire for 'regular church services and a suitable edifice'. In February 1888 McGregor Chalmers was appointed architect for the project and the following May the foundation stone was laid. Built of red sandstone from Locharbriggs, the church opened in February 1889 as a mission church and in May was granted the status of a Chapel of Ease. In July 1890 it was disjoined and created a parish, *quoad sacra*. The west aisle was added in 1899 and the east aisle in 1925.

The houses and corn mill at Crookston. The mill was first established in the late eighteenth century and the operation included cottages and kailyards for the workers. The mill wheel was powered by a lade run from the White Cart Water and the mill's products were then transported to market along the Glasgow, Paisley and Johnstone Canal. These buildings were demolished around 1958 and the area's past is reflected in the names of the streets built there – Moulin (French for mill) Terrace and Lade Terrace.

Three Mile House, Cardonald.

This is not Three-Mile House at Halfway, but Three Mile Cottage which was situated three miles from Paisley. Hillington Road South now meets Paisley Road West at this point and a row of shops stretches eastwards. Such a peaceful scene has long been a thing of the past.

Albion buses were popular mainly with the larger bus fleets such as Young's of Paisley or John Sword's 'Midland' bus service of Airdrie. This 24-seater of 1925 belonged to the latter company and ran through Cardonald in competition with the Glasgow Corporation's tram services from Glasgow to Paisley, which were extended to Johnstone in the mid-1920s.

Another typical mid-1920s motor bus which operated on the services running through Cardonald between Glasgow and Paisley. This was a Vulcan of 1924, owned by Urquhart of Paisley, and is pictured with the driver George Galbraith, in the town's King Street. It is possible that this bus was about to run on a special service to the Highland Show at Bellahouston Park.

Two No. 22 trams on Paisley Road West pass each other at the foot of Corkerhill Road in May 1952.

The Old Toll House on Crookston Road, *c.* 1910. A map of 1858 shows that a weighing machine stood behind the toll and presumably this was used to work out charges for loaded carts.

Crookston Road.

Amongst other things, this corner shop on Crookston Road provided teas, ices, newspapers and a circulating library. The view dates from around 1935 and tramlines had not yet been carried on into Crookston Road for the terminus.

Cart Bridge, Crookston.

Crookston Road crosses over the White Cart Water by the Howford Bridge, seen here in a very sylvan setting. It ran through the large estate owned by the Ross family of Hawkhead Castle which was carved up when Hawkhead Hospital was built, at that time well out in the country, on the western side of the road. The grounds on the eastern side were opened to the public as Rosshall Park in 1965. When the bridge was replaced by a more substantial structure in the early 1930s, Crookston Road had to be realigned at this point.

The Old Toll House and Castle, Crookston Road.

Another toll house, this time about halfway up Crookston Road. This view was taken outside what is now the entrance to Leverndale Hospital. Before Brockburn Road was built to give access to the council houses in the Pollok scheme, this road was very short and only led to the isolated castle and the farm opposite it.

Crookston Castle was built by Sir Alexander Stewart in the late fourteenth century. A tower house standing in a dry ditch, it took the site of an earlier wooden castle which had been built by Robert Croc, an important retainer of the House of Stewart, in 1202. The building was rectangular and had four square corner towers of which only the north-eastern remains, although the vaulted base of the south-east tower is still standing. It was surrounded by an oval-shaped fosse or ditch about forty feet wide. This was probably a dry ditch with spikes or pales and the castle appears to have been enclosed by a stone wall and was entered from the west by a drawbridge across the fosse. The basement is still there. In the fifteenth century the castle became the seat of the Earls of Lennox, the first of whom was Sir John Stewart of Darnley who assumed the title around 1473. The castle was badly damaged after a siege in 1489 and was then left to decay. The last known date of habitation was 1562 when it was the home of Charles, sixth Earl of Lennox and brother of Lord Darnley, husband of Mary, Queen of Scots.

The pictures here and on the facing page show Lamington Road when it was known as Lennox Road.. By the early 1920s, Glasgow had annexed so many of its surrounding villages and burghs that many street names were duplicated. This was causing so much confusion, especially for postal deliveries, that it was decided to eliminate the duplication by renaming some of the streets.

Completed in the early 1930s, the new names were taken mostly from Scottish towns and villages. Other new street names in Cardonald were Crookston Avenue, previously Carlton Gardens; Cardonald Gardens, previously Edward Gardens; Blairgowrie Road, previously Comrie Road; Talla Road, previously Erskine Road; Queensland Drive, previously Woodhall Drive; Walkerburn Road, previously Ross Avenue; and Berwick Drive, previously Roxburgh Circus.

This firm moved from Hutchesontown to Cardonald in 1900 and manufactured safety, reducing and stop valves, tubular steel barrows, spiral springs and, later, first class marine and land mountings of all descriptions. The man in the back row with the collar, tie, and heavy moustache was possibly the foreman. Beside him in a bowler hat and stiff high collar could have been the owner.

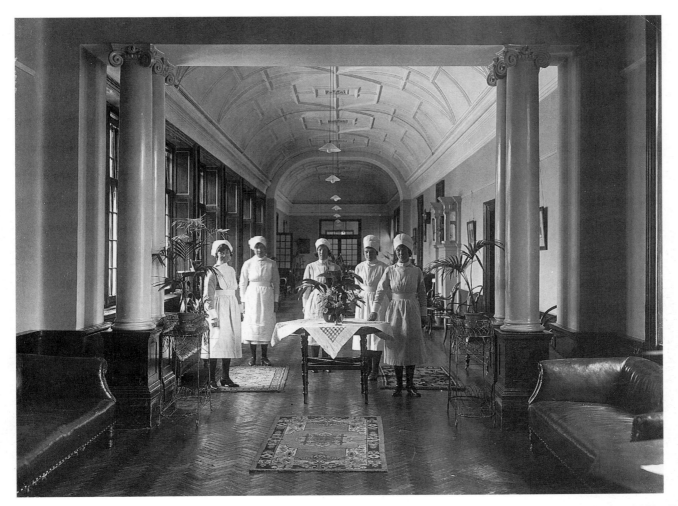

Govan Parochial Board set up asylum accommodation for 36 patients in their poorhouse in Eglinton Street, Glasgow, in the late 1850s. Patients were transferred in 1872 to the new asylum in Merryflats Poorhouse which stood on the site of the present Southern General Hospital. By the late 1880s the new Govan District Lunacy Board had to consider building a new asylum. The site chosen was Hawkhead, a large country estate and by 1896 the new asylum buildings had been built. This picture shows an indoor airing court where patients could exercise in bad weather.

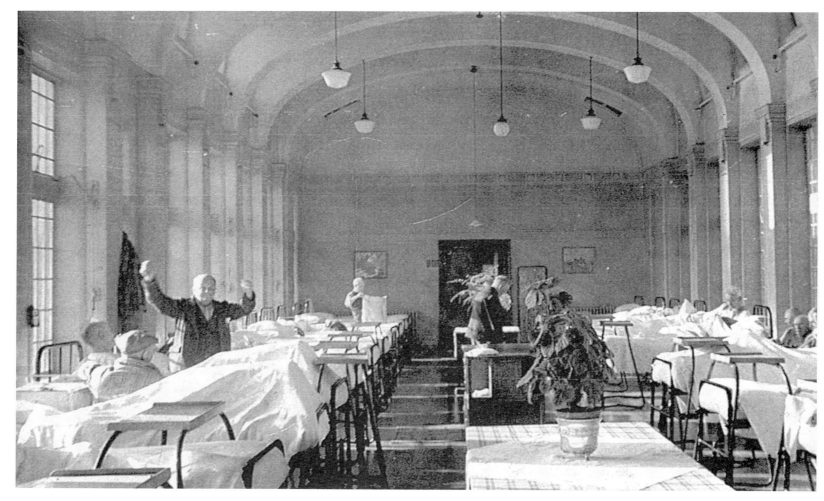

Other facilities for the patients included in the 1890s a farm with a dairy herd, byre and poultry house. As well as working on the farm, patients helped lay out the grounds before and after the asylum was built. They created ornamental plots, planted shrubs and trees, built fences and laid roads. About 1929 the building became Hawkhead Mental Hospital and was renamed Leverndale Hospital in 1964. A 200-seat chapel for all denominations was created out of the old asylum dining hall in 1963. This is one of the hospital's Solarium wards.

MOSSPARK DRIVE LOOKING WEST

Mosspark Farm stood on the outskirts of Cardonald before Glasgow's first council housing estate was built in the area after the First World War.

Mosspark Boulevard is very wide at this section and as well as a road for general traffic, a reserved track was provided for the trams. The No.3 white tram ran from here through the city to the University. There are also signs that construction work on the track had not yet been completed.

The Railway Institute, Corkerhill. Until 1896, Corkerhill was merely a junction on the Canal Line between Bellahouston and Crookston but thanks to the enterprise of the Glasgow & South Western Railway Co. it became a suburb of Glasgow, as they erected houses there to accommodate their engine drivers, stokers, fitters and others who worked in the engine shed. For the population of six hundred, 122 houses were built along with a hall for three hundred, plus a reading room and a library. Later, Glasgow Corporation housing was built in the area.

A postcard captioned 'The Old Roman Bridge, Corkerhill'. I have not seen any mention of a bridge in the area dating from Roman times, but on a map of 1904 there is a bridge marked over the river five miles due west of Corkerhill called Roma or Rona Bridge.

Crookston Road leads from Paisley Road West through Crookston to Barrhead Road at the Hurlet, seen here *c.* 1905.

NITSHILL FROM THE STATION

From the Hurlet, Barrhead Road leads west to Paisley and east to the old village of Nitshill, seen here in the mid-1920s.

The Levern Church and Hall, Nitshill. The village owes its existence chiefly to neighbouring coal mines and quarries which were established in the nineteenth century. Other industries which employed the locals in that period included a chemical works which was established in 1807.

Wardhill Farm, Nitshill.